MW01441170

Essence Of Conservation

North County High School
10 E. 1st Avenue
Glen Burnie, MD 21061
Volume 4
2023-2024
Cavalry

Table of Contents

Title	Author	Type	Page
Roses' Prose	Rose Dorsch	Poem	
Arising Fall	Kelli Bennett	Poem	1
Apartment 301	Bryce Densmore	Short Story	3
Just Like You	Alivia Houghling	Poem	7
Found	Rose Dorsch	Poem	9
Our Book	Serena Morin	Poem	13
Tranquility	Dakota Locklear	Poem	17
Crusade	Serena Morin	Poem	18
Unbroken	Kendyl Adair	Poem	20
As the Days Go By	Anonymous	Poem	21
Drift	Sydney Jones	Poem	29
What I Deserve	Anonymous	Poem	31
Decay	Rose Dorsch	Poem	35
My Bones	Serena Morin	Poem	37
Consumption	Victoria Cameron	Poem	38
Summative of Lord of the Flies	Demitri Figueroa	Essay	39
One Pager	Erika Ochonogor	One Pager	41
Chapter	Serena Morin	Poem	44
Homelessness	Diamond Kumani	Essay	47
Distance	Serena Morin	Poem	50
Advisor Letter	Victoria Cameron		
Staff Page	Staff		
Philosophy	Staff		
Art Doodle Credits	Staff		

Joshua Tree	Victoria Cameron	Photography	Break
Tiger	Chloe Heslop	Drawing	2
Flower Through Pain	Victoria Cameron	Photography	4
Octopus	Angel Jimenez	Drawing	8
Small Beauty	Victoria Cameron	Photography	12
Squid	Angel Jimenez	Drawing	14
Lovely Lily	Victoria Cameron	Photography	Break
Fish	Angel Jimenez	Drawing	19
Clown Fish	Angel Jimenez	Drawing	Break
Forgotten	Victoria Cameron	Photography	Break
Skeleton Stingray	Angel Jimenez	Drawing	30
Masks	Layla White	Drawing	32
Dead Shark	Angel Jimenez	Drawing	33
Tortured	Saige Gunning	Drawing	34
Pig Head	Monire Rugibi	Drawing	40
Ralph	Erika Ochonogor	Drawing	42
LOTF	Bao-Thy Nguyen	Drawing	43
Among the Green	Cherish Brown	Photography	Break
The Melting Face	Ryan Fonjock	Drawing	49
Coral Bells	Victoria Cameron	Photography	Break
No Title Given	Buka Ragu	Mixed Media	Philosophy

Art Doodle Credits

Waverly Boyer	Trigger Warning, 1, 2, 3, 6, 11, 13, 17, 18, 21, 34, 35, 37, 44, 50
Emily Gonzalez	9, 18, 22
Angel Jimenez	48
Saige Gunning	36 and pollution spots

Trigger Warnings

Death
Depression
Suicide
Blood
Homelessness

Rose's Prose

"My wish is to stay always like this,
Living quietly in a corner of nature."
– Claude Monet

This school year has been full of ups and downs. The magazine has been a victim in comparison to previous years where work was somewhat more accessible. The theme we landed on was the progression of nature, as well as climate change. The state of our world has been called into question.

This year was an interesting one when it came to being on the staff, but we managed to scrape through.

"Wherever I roam, nature is the only stranger that feels like home." – Angie Welland-Crosby

Joshua Tree, Victoria Cameron, Photography

Arising Fall

Kelli Bennett

Green fading into yellow,
Then ember, then red,
I've always felt mellow
As Autumn peeked its head.

Limitless blue skies,
Dusk's mesmerizing abyss
Enough to fog my eyes
With droplets of pure-bliss.

There's a chill in the air,
Clothing me in familiar tingles.
The breeze caresses and combs through my hair,
A warmth inside me somehow rekindled.

The bold sun illuminates the leaves,
Weaving its way through heavenly cotton.
The land, the shore, and all that breathes
Are embraced by its rays, not forgotten.

And as the leaves age and wrinkle up and fall in decay,
I'll watch with contentment, awaiting next year's replay.

Tiger, Chloe Heslop, Drawing

Apartment 301

Bryce Densmore

Alyssa closed the car door, her heels echoing against the deserted pavement. The looming apartment complex stood overhead, its silhouette swallowed by thick, swirling clouds that veiled the moonlight. Empty streets echoed with a ghostly silence, interrupted only by the distant hum of nearby streetlights. Alyssa's steps quickened as she sensed the irregular rhythm of footsteps—sometimes louder, sometimes fading, yet no one was in sight. She hurried toward her apartment building, seeking refuge in the warm, beckoning glow of the lobby. A young man manned the front desk, his presence offering a sense of comfort. She waved a greeting before pressing the elevator button, anticipating its arrival.

Beside her, an older man approached, his clean-shaven appearance contrasting with an unsettling air about him. "Late night for a young lady like yourself," he remarked in a soft but oddly piercing voice.

"Working overtime," Alyssa replied, a shiver running down her spine, her grip tightening on her bag.

"Be careful," the man warned with a disconcerting smile. "These streets are dangerous for a lady like you." The elevator chimed, Alyssa swiftly stepped inside, her unease mounting as the man entered but pressed no floor button.

As the elevator ascended, the atmosphere grew stifling. Alyssa took a step back, trying to distance herself from the man's presence. The elevator abruptly halted, its doors sliding open. Alyssa exited, her heart racing, and hurried down the narrow hallway toward her door. Glancing back, she found the man had vanished.

Fumbling for her keys, she unlocked the door, stepping into the darkness of her apartment, the feeling of being watched intensifying. She shut the door behind her, the click of the lock offering little comfort in the suffocating silence.

Alyssa flicked the light switch, her cozy yet eerily silent apartment unfolding before her. She hung her black coat on the hook, releasing a sigh as she discarded her heels among the clutter of other shoes in the corner. A sense of unease lingered as she undid her ponytail, letting her hair fall loosely around her shoulders.

Moving into the small kitchen, she deposited her purse on the counter and retrieved the leftover pizza from the fridge. The microwave hummed ominously as she warmed it, the only audible sound in her otherwise silent abode.

In the other room, she turned on the television, and was greeted by eerie reruns of "The Twilight Zone," the episode depicting a haunting hitchhiker amplifying the tension in the room. The microwave beeped, and Alyssa transferred the slices to the coffee table.

Suddenly, a sharp knock echoed through the apartment, causing Alyssa to pause, her heart thudding in her chest. After a moment's hesitation, she approached the door, cautiously peering through the peephole, and finding an empty hallway.

Unlocking the door, Alyssa discovered an unexpected bouquet of flowers and a card lying at her doorstep. She scanned the area for any sign of the sender but found nothing. Her brows furrowed

Flower Through Pain, Victoria Cameron, Photography

in discomfort as she brought the bouquet inside, her fingers trembling slightly as she opened the card.

Inside was an anniversary message, chillingly vague: "Missing you already. Can't wait for our next encounter." Alyssa's unease deepened, a shiver running down her spine as she tossed the card in the trash, unnerved by the unsettling message.

The apartment felt more oppressive now, shadows seemingly flickering in her periphery. Alyssa couldn't shake off the feeling that something was amiss, that an unwelcome presence lingered around her.

Alyssa sank back onto the couch, attempting to distract herself from the unsettling feeling gripping her. The TV droned on, its sound reduced to a mere murmur in the background, unable to drown out her growing anxiety. She couldn't shake off the chilling thought: why her?

A sudden movement caught her attention—a swift blur by the window. Her heart skipped a beat, adrenaline surging through her veins. Alyssa inched toward the window, her breath shallow and rapid. Peering out, she saw nothing but the empty rooftop, the vast darkness enveloping her building.

Swiftly shutting the blinds, Alyssa refused to leave anything to chance. The uneasy feeling gnawed at her, urging her to take precautions. With a sense of foreboding, she tried to distract herself

> "The words sent shivers down Alyssa's spine the stalker's voice alarmingly close"

by moving around the apartment, but the sense of being watched persisted, growing more suffocating with each passing second.

Fatigue weighed heavily upon her shoulders, prompting her retreat to the bedroom. As she entered the room, the lights flickered and abruptly died out, enveloping her in an oppressive darkness. Alyssa's heart raced; she knew the power box outside her apartment must have tripped again.

Reaching for a flashlight, she turned to confront the darkness, but her movements halted abruptly. A stark silhouette loomed on the balcony, barely discernible against the moonlit night. Fear gripped her, urging her into action.

Snatching her cellphone from her purse, Alyssa's heart pounded in her chest. The figure's sudden movement rattled the balcony door handle. Panic surged through her veins as she sprinted for safety, dashing into the bedroom and seeking refuge.

With trembling hands, she squeezed into the closet, burying herself among the clothes. Silence engulfed the room, save for the rapid thudding of her heart. The stalker's ominous presence lingered outside.

She fumbled with her phone, dialing the emergency number. "Please, help," she whispered, her voice quivering with fear as she relayed her address, her words desperate and barely audible.

Alyssa's heart pounded against her chest as she clutched her phone, her breaths shallow and panicked. The abrupt end of the call left her in a chilling silence, her senses on high alert.

Then, amidst the eerie silence of the night, she heard it—the faint creak of her porch door sliding open. Terror gripped her, paralyzing her with fear as the stalker's deliberate footsteps echoed through the empty apartment, their presence hauntingly real.

The footsteps halted, plunging the room into an ominous stillness. Alyssa held her breath, her heart hammering in her chest. Had the stalker left? Was she alone?

A sudden squeak shattered the silence—a dining room chair moving. The hair on the back of Alyssa's neck stood on end. What were they doing? The chilling realization sank in—they were searching for her.

The footsteps resumed, growing louder, signaling the stalker's movement through the apartment. Every step echoed with malevolence, every sound magnified in the oppressive silence.

Then, a voice, cold and menacing, sliced through the air. "Pretty girl, where are you hiding?" The words sent shivers down Alyssa's spine, the stalker's voice alarmingly close.

The footsteps approached, the floorboards creaking just beside her hiding spot. Alyssa's breath hitched, her heart threatening to burst from her chest. A looming shadow outlined the closet door, sending a wave of terror coursing through her veins.

Her hand flew to her mouth, attempting to silence her ragged breaths. The stalker paused, the air thick with foreboding. Alyssa's eyes widened in terror as the stalker's hand reached for the closet door, the loud squeak piercing the suffocating silence. As the stalker opened the door slowly, Alyssa braced for an inevitable confrontation.

"Found you." The man hissed, shattering the silence. Alyssa instantly recognized him, it was the man from the elevator—the unsettling stranger from earlier. There was no time for regret, only survival instincts kicking in.

In an instant, he seized her arm, forcefully hurling her to the floor outside the closet, clutching a stolen kitchen knife tightly in his grip. His twisted grin loomed over Alyssa as she lay defenseless on the ground. The glint of the blade inched closer to her face, a twisted grin on his face.

"You have such a pretty face. I won't damage it too badly," he hissed. He dragged the knife along her face, lightly grazing her cheek, drawing a thin line that began to trickle blood. Tears streamed down Alyssa's face, mixing with the dread and pain.

Suddenly, the piercing sound of police sirens and the flashing lights of blue and red echoed through the apartment. The stalker's demeanor shifted momentarily, a flash of alarm passing over his face. He swiftly regained his composure, realizing he had little time. With a hasty retreat, he bolted outside, vanishing into the obscurity of the night.

The aftermath blurred into a haze for Alyssa—images of shattered doors, frantic police inquiries, and the subsequent investigation into the man's identity. Amidst the chaos, the unsettling truth of the stalker's escape lingered, casting a long, haunting shadow over Alyssa's fragile sense of security.

Just Like You

Alivia Houghtling

As a kid I was always told
Slow Down, Be quiet, Keep Calm
I grew up knowing what an IQ was
it was printed in the back of my mind
Being labeled
Special Ed
You can't Read
You can't write
You can't spell
Slow Down, Be quiet, Keep Calm
The other kids would say she only passed because she got special help
Even though I passed all by myself
I would laugh a little hard or talk a little bit too much and play a little too long
So they told me
Slow Down, Be quiet, Keep Calm
As middle school happenend I would hear laughing and giggling from my classmates when it was my turn to Read
Spend days arguing with friends because they couldn't understand why I couldn't do my own homeowrk
And when I talked it was annoying
Slow Down, Be quiet, Keep Calm

I can't Read
I can't write
I can't spell
But the tides have turned and the tables have shitfted it's always now
Hurry up
Speak UP
Still Keep Calm
I have learned to Read five paragraphs ahead when its my turn to Read
Resight
Resight
Resight
I'm sick of being defined because of my IQ
I can't Read
I can't write
I can't spell
But yet I'm still human just like you

Octopus, Angel Jimenez, Drawing

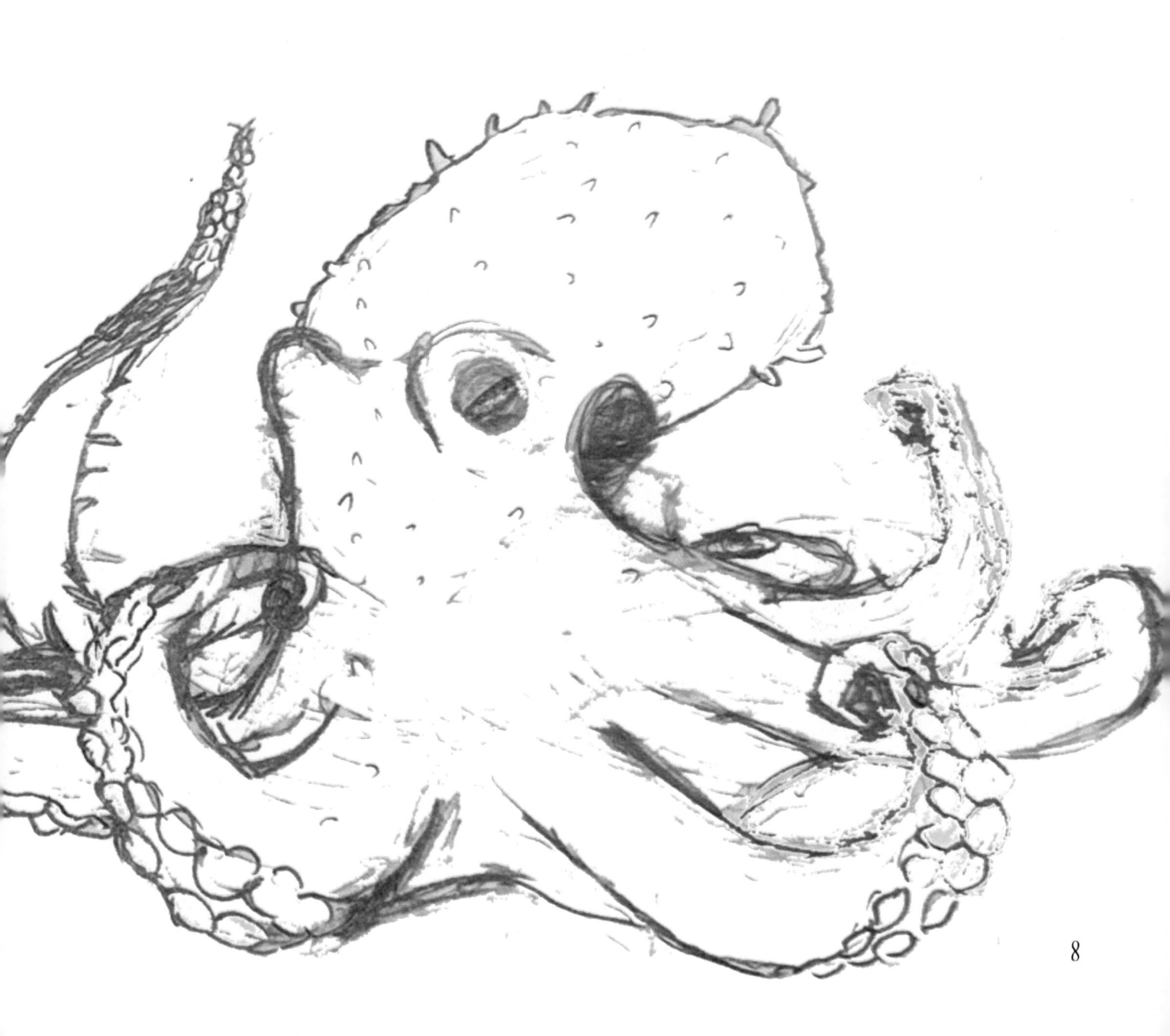

Found

Rose Dorsch

you can give a piece of your soul, fracture your spirit and still be whole.

that's love after all, lending it out
allowing it to bleed and fill with doubt.

we all have different amounts, so upon the opportunity we wait to pounce.

I've done it 4 times...only 2 still have it
don't exactly wanna hand it out to whoever wants to grab it.

one raised me and fell down a hole, thought he'd always have it but it feels like he stole.

one saw my soul when it was jet dark, she saw my beast slobber and bark..
she ran away and told me to slay it..
waited so long to finally say it..

one left me shattered, one left me tattered, one made me sad, one made me feel I've been had.

yet, 2 remain that lifted a weight, caught my fall like a cushion on slate.

as my quarters turned flimsy and my life was uprooted, my mental state was cataclysmically booted.

my everything fell and I'm still falling beside it, I wish I was better, and could hide it.

one came along, from across a screen, and lended herself in a way I hadn't seen.

She cared, listened, and tried her best, helping me feel a bit more at rest.

I didn't grow up with a mother, but she proceeded to do, making a pandemic able to be gotten through.

She's got a piece and it was one worth giving, as it filled a gap that made for easier living.

one I swear was fated to be, no other explanation for how they met me.

hearing their words in the hall that spoke out, as I was filled with then recent doubt.

Something in me whispered "talk" and subsequently my feet began to walk.

So I did and it was nice, never did I even think twice.

but something began to become apparent, that they helped make my life coherent.

things I loved, they did too, listening when I was blue.

but she did the same, was I doing it again, did I deserve the blame?
yet it never came, waiting felt like a game.

ironically on that 10 pm night, when one extinguished my ability to see her light, they shined theirs and once again made my life bright.

and ever since, they've had that chunk and being around them removes my funk.

none of my idiosyncrasies around them ever seem to inconvenience me, no mood shift to ever sudden sequence me.

the other day, there was a discrepancy, but small and was talked through with me.

anxiety took over and I lost control, the twitching began, I shook like a bowl.

they realized why, and saw myself lone, then decided to get off the phone.

I explained what was going on despite my best efforts, I was trying so hard it made my head hurt.

but they saw what was causing it, and placed their hands onto mine, vowing to never let it happen another time.

few ever have done so with me, to let the world fade and let a moment become reality.

I felt seen, heard, and loved...not ignored and left to be shoved.

I'm so happy I let myself let people into my heart again, a late arrival mom and a best friend.

It's hard opening up to a possible conflict, like using a DVD that doesn't always play a disc, but when that disc works and it runs brisk, it was all worth it, to take that risk.

Small Beauty, Victoria Cameron, Photography

Our Book

Serena Morin

The things i'd do to always keep you
You mean the world to me
So i write every line about you
I could write silly little books about you
Just to read them to you
So you know how I truly feel
And you might think
My book would have a chapter for you
But I don't see you as a chapter in my book
I see you as the title
You made me realize my life truly is a book
And my book will always end with you

Squid, Angel Jimenez, Drawing

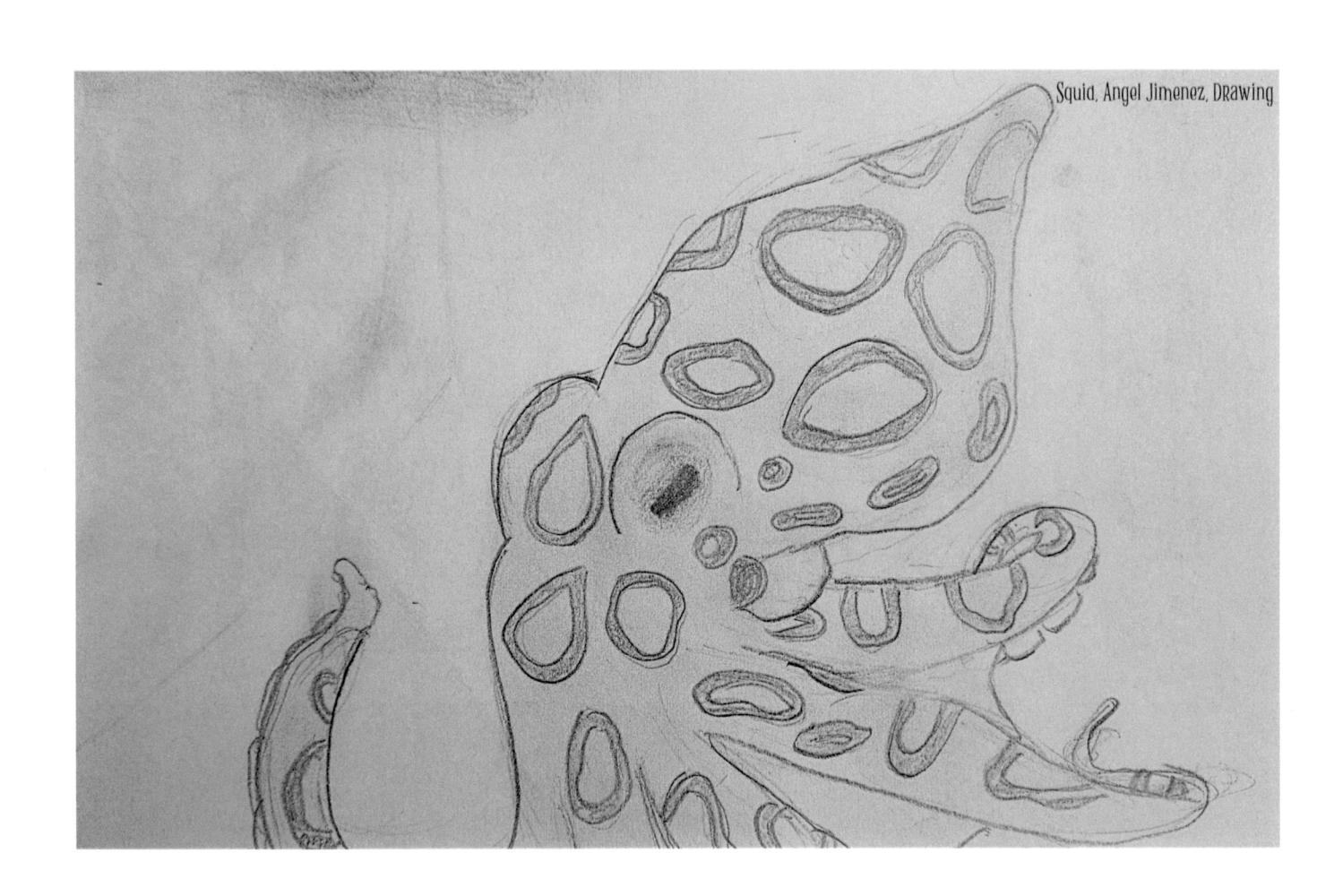

"Nature always wears the colors of the spirit." – Ralph Waldo Emerson

Lovely Lily, Victoria Cameron, Photography

Tranquility

Dakota Locklear

There's something comforting yet familiar
about the coldness of a place that's supposed
to be bursting with life.
Looking out onto the frost paved concrete,
Sometimes unforgiving, I feel more at home with it.
I embrace the cold, the quiet.
Right as dawn breaks and the earth awakens,
I often imagine this cycle as life.
But not in the same way you might think.
All it takes is the sun to wake up the earth,
But what makes the earth awaken is the orbit.
What makes you orbit?
What makes your earth awaken?
For everyone, it's diverse.
The coldness of the frost paved concrete could be a heart,
Cold, fragile, and bitter.
But then, as the sun arises, even if cloudy life sprouts from
What seems like nothing.

The sunrise is the life being fueled into the cold fragile heart,
Just to be torn into coldness.
Some nights are colder than others,

But what happens always?
The sun arises again.
This is how life is.
The sun always rises again.

Crusade

Serena Morin

My life with you is like an endless crusade
I'd do anything for you in a way
I'd change everything I know for you
My political views
My social views
My Religious views
All to be with you
All to just have you
All to ride with you on this crazy crusade
Others say it's wrong
The same way we think it's right
I'm willing to fight for our love
I've never met someone who shines this bright
You light up my world
So it never feels like night
I know I got something on this ride right
And it's having you by my side

Fish, Angel Jimenez, Drawing

Unbroken
Kendyl Adair

Do not kiss the lips of the broken,
do not miss the hips of the spoken,
A gentle finger glides upon broken glass,
The blood will pass,
Bleeding onto my fingers,
Soaking until it lingers,
Shushed by the important,
Hushed by the unspoken.

As the Days Go By
Anonymous

As the days go by, I still sleep until noon
I sleep away my feelings because I don't know what to do
do I talk to someone? or do I let the wounds bloom?
there's a whole bunch of people, but i feel alone in this room
i pick myself up everytime that i fall
because i know that sometimes i be down for too long
it hurts knowing i can't express to people how i feel
which means they'll never know how to deal
to deal with me, to deal with my feelings
to deal with everything and remain still here
still here with me, in the end it's nobody that i see
every time things go wrong they always seem to leave
to leave me, my feelings, my heart, and my mind
leaving looking for something to find
to find why they left or where they gonna go
but i can't find answers, i never seem to know

Large Octopus, Angel Jimenez, Drawing

"Where flowers bloom so does hope." – Ladybird Johnson

Clown Fish, Angel Jimenez, Drawing

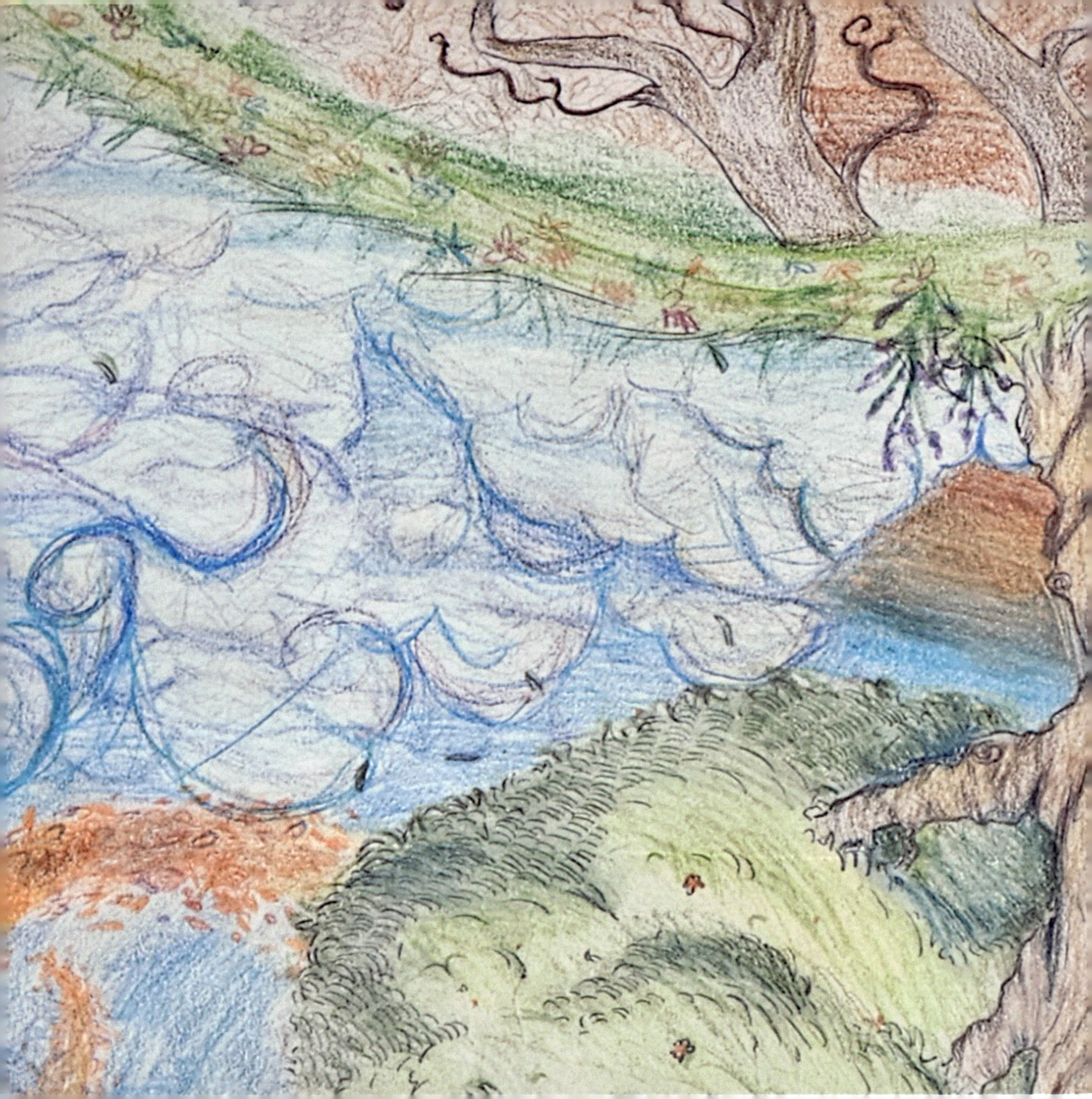

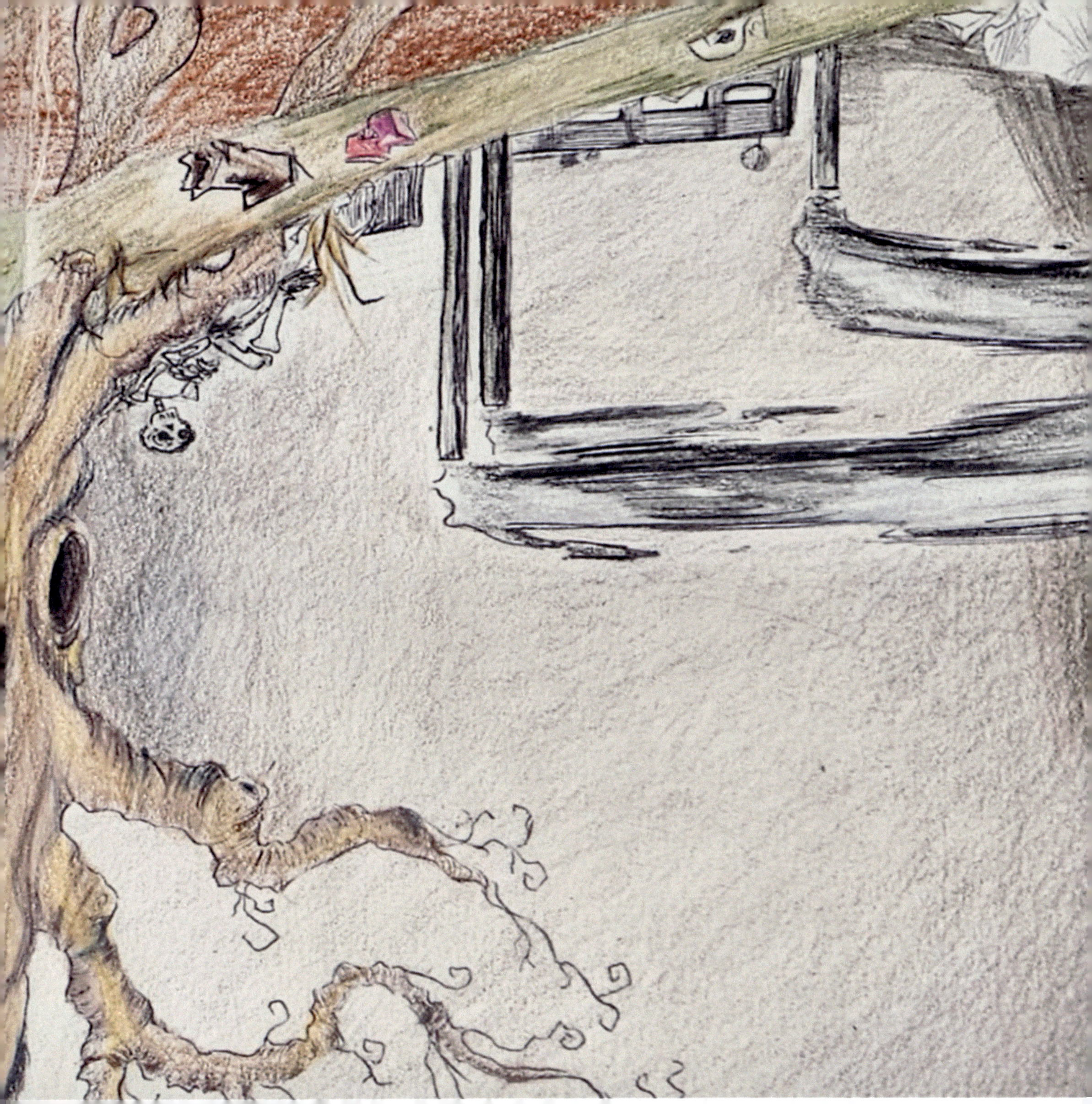

"Sunsets are proof that endings can often be beautiful, too." – Beau Taplin

Forgotten. Victoria Cameron. Photography

Drift

Sydeny Jones

Sometimes you don't always end up with a happy ending, but there is an ending to everything. Ultimately, we all become stories, memories, something that once was. Knowing this makes it seem meaningless to express loneliness.

People brush past me as they walk by. They had no intention of touching me, but I find it comforting to pretend their presence is similar to company. So many people walk through these halls, yet their eyes are vacant. everyone was so disconnected, but now I think I was too.

I have no importance to those around me. I've always felt out of place. I've lived through the lives of others, and socializing feels like a waste. This loneliness often makes me feel as if I'm sinking, but in a way, I am in full control of.

I feel like a ship that was ill-equipped for open water, yet I still abandoned the harbor and crashed into the open sea. The waves pull me in, as I try to reach a destination this ship I am, is just not made to reach. Waves come and go, rise and fall, but now it feels like they continuously pull me in.

 Instead of returning to safety, I continue to let myself float out further into the secluded, deep body of water. Slowly drowning in a sea of countless thoughts. I wanted nothing more but to be seen, heard, or anything. I was the ocean, they wanted rivers. I shined like the moon, while they longed for stars. As the sun rises, the moon disappears, and again I'm stuck in this dismal hallway. Slowly but surely everything, once again has gone grey.

Skeleton Stingray, Angel Jimenez, Drawing

What I Deserve

Anonymous

i don't deserve this
to cry at night holding myself
wondering when things are gonna be alright
all the nights when i couldn't even sleep
making me feel like if i talk about my feelings then i'm weak
questioning myself, not knowing if i'm pretty
looking at the other girl, thinking i look silly
feeling like i'm not enough and wondering what i'm doing wrong
god i just want to get better why is the process taking so long?
alone is what you feel when you're not around people
or maybe it's what you feel all the time
i could tell you how i feel alone
but you wouldn't wanna hear about mine
i hurt in silence and be happy in public
my time is coming and i don't wanna hear nothing
i be there for everybody, but who's gonna be there for me?
i asked a question but there's no hands that i see
she cries in her room but tells everybody she's okay
who's going to save her before something's taken away
you made me feel like i needed validation
but i wanna tell you that's false information
you hurt me and you just kept going
like an old bandaid that won't hold on
she tried to take her life away and didn't care about the future
all the pain you've caused me: i don't need you...you're not a suture.

Masks, Layla White, Drawing

Dead Shark, Angel Jimenez, Drawing

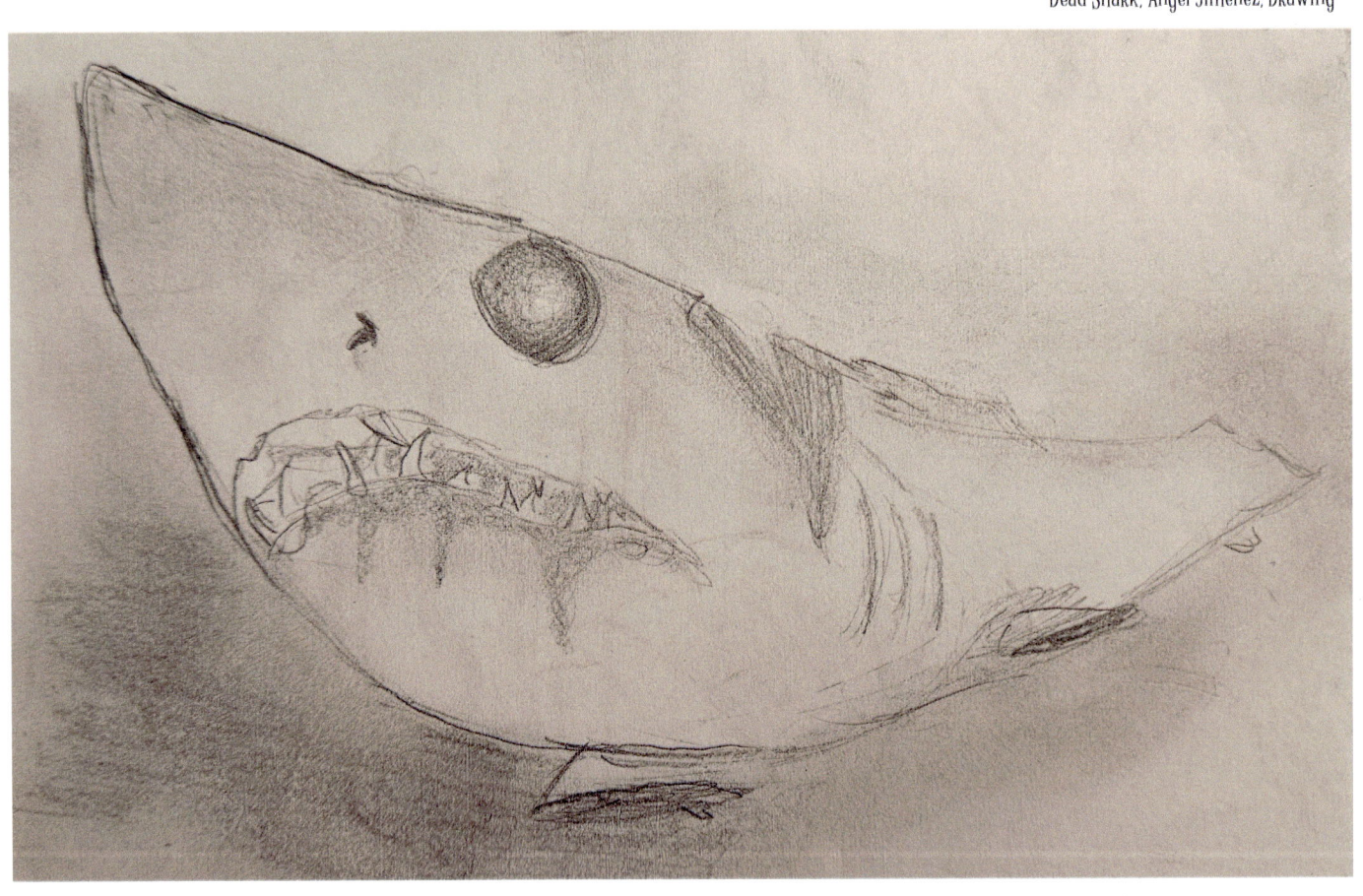

Tortured, Saige Gunning, Drawing

Decay
Rose Dorsch

Everything, walks the road, everything will soon erode.

Time dusts off, mass and atoms
Destroys all that we can fathom

People, plants, we age and die
We don't quite know the reason why

Turn to ash and fade away
Nothing more there is to say

But that does not mean we need to fret
Upon this journey we all set

The state of a fate should not decide,
what we do, and make us hide

We should care even more than we do
Knowing what we'll eventually go through

We are valuable, because we do not stay
We are valuable because we'll soon decay

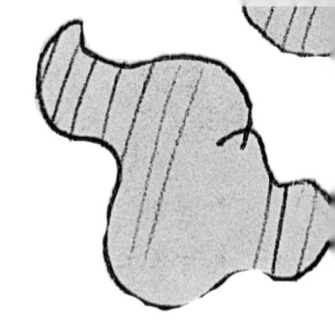

"We should care even more than we do"

My Bones

Serena Morin

I'd break all my bones for you
In my head you would do the same for me too
But in reality we both know that isn't true
I'd tumble, fall, and dislocate every bone in me
Just to see you
Just to feel you
Just to know your bones are okay
While mine suffer and fray
I don't care if in the end my bones aren't fine
I'll stand back up and be alright
As long as i know your bones are safe

"Just to know your bones are okay"

Consumption

Victoria Cameron

You hear about the loss

of appetite
of will
of sleep
of hope

Things that grow like moss
drowning under hydrogen
and oxygen walls
this growing amalgamation
of before and now;
a neon sign for sale

an emptiness that needs
filling
Repaired in pieces by a
gluttonous fire;

Consumption Ruins
it stalls
it breaks down will
and helps put up walls

as if the act of growing fat
could ever bring you back;

Consumption

"as if
 the act
  of growing fat

could ever
   bring you
     back."

Summative of Lord of the Flies

Demitri Figueroa

What would happen if a group of kids were stranded on an island and were forced to create their own civilization? That's right, just kids making a complete order system with multiple jobs on an island nobody knows. Well that's the main plot of Lord of The Flies by William Golding. The story goes as is: a couple of kids survived a plane crash and are stranded on an unknown island. The kids at first celebrate the feeling of no adults, but then as time flies, they realize the dangers of the island and experience problems with keeping authority. In this certain story, the theme "survival of the fittest" is best represented by William Golding's usage of literary elements.

One type of literary element Golding uses was characterization. There are many different times in the story when Golding used this element. Such as when describing Piggy, Ralph, or any of the characters. The following quotes are an example, "A thing was crawling out of the forest. It came darkly, uncertainty. Simon was crying out something about a dead man on a hill. The beast was on its knees in the center, its arms folded over its face. It was crying out against the abominable noise, something about a body on the hill. The crowd surged after it, poured down the rock, leapt on to the beast, screamed, struck, bit, tore. Simon's dead body moved out toward the open sea." The quote explains two perspectives; a boy named Simon and the boys he was trying to talk to. From Simon's perspective, he was about to tell the boys about a dead man on the hill. While from the others' perspective, Simon looked like a darkened beast crawling toward them. This then causes the crowd to beat up Simon and kill him, causing his dead body to be out at sea. Golding used characterization in Simon by making him appear monstrous to the other boys, causing him to lose his life, thus the characterization in Simon's death best represents the theme "survival of the fittest".

Another literary element Golding used is Symbolism. The main symbols in Lord of The Flies are the fire, the conch, or a murder of a pig. That symbolism is shown in the following excerpt, "...prodding with his spear whenever pigflesh appeared. Jack was on top of the sow, stabbing downward with his knife. Roger found a lodgement for his point and began to push till he was leaning with his whole weight. Then Jack found the throat and the hot blood spouted over his hands. The sow collapsed under them. He giggled and flicked them while the boys laughed at his reeking palms." In the excerpt, Jack and his group of boys have finally captured a pig, and now they are stabbing it, poking it, and killing it with their weapons. Once Jack has killed the pig, he shows the boys his bloody hands and they all laugh – not caring about the brutality of the hunt or the poor sow itself. This symbol – the sow's death – represents savagery and how the boys choose hunting in order to survive in their environment. The boys' behavior shows the theme of "survival of the fittest," whereas they adapted to their environment by hunting animals.

The final literary element used by Golding is Text Structure. Again, there are many examples of the usage of text structure. However, this example best represents this theme, "Beneath the smoke was a dot that might be a funnel. The fire was dead. They saw that straightaway; saw what they had really known down on the beach when the smoke of home had beckoned. The fire was out, smokeless and dead; the watchers were gone. They let the bloody fire go out." In the Lord of The Flies, the fire represented escape and created smoke for ships to see and rescue the boys. However, just as a ship was near them, their signal was burned out and the ship went away. This also causes Ralph to realize the reason this happened — the hunters were supposed to watch the fire. But instead they went out hunting and let the fire go out. This type of text structure included much description about the event and shows how because of the fire going out, the boys did not escape the island. Thus, they were not fit for survival at the time due to having no signal.

By using literary elements such as characterization, symbolism and text structure, William Golding is able to show a clear theme in Lord of The Flies. Simon's death, Jack's tribe hunting the pig, and the fire going out just as a ship comes by are all examples of elements Golding uses to represent the theme "Survival of the Fittest." Although this theme can also be shown using different literary elements rather than the three mentioned, they are the types of elements that are shown again and again throughout the course of the story and, thus, helps the reader know what theme Golding is trying to tell them.

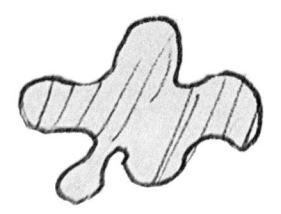

Pig Head, Monike Rugibi, Drawing

LORD of the FLIES
Chapters 1 and 2

By: Erikha Ochonogor

PIGGY

- Intellectual
- Full of thoughts
- Unfit
- "He was shorter than the fair boy and very fat" pg 1
- "Piggy took off his shoes and socks, arranged them carefully on the ledge, and tested the water with one toe" Pg 13

THEME

- During desperate times, take charge.
- "Seems to me we ought to have a chief to decide things. A chief! A chief! I ought to be chief." Pg 22
- We are better together
- "Everybody must stay round here and wait and not go away. If we talk more we'd get mixed and lose each other." Pg 23

Ralph, Erika Ochonogor, Drawing

43

LOFF. Bao-Thy Nguyen, Drawing

Chapter
Serena Morin

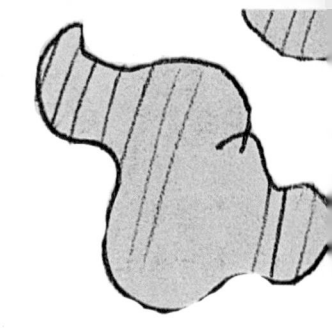

I want to believe you're still here with me
Even though you have been gone for a while
I look at your pictures and remember
Your beautiful smile
How tender your touch
All of your love
Then i remember how long you've been gone
How sad i was when you first left
How I've grown and become strong
How happy i've become now
Even though you're gone
Your chapter is over in my book
But I can't bring myself to flip the page

"Your chapter is over in my book"

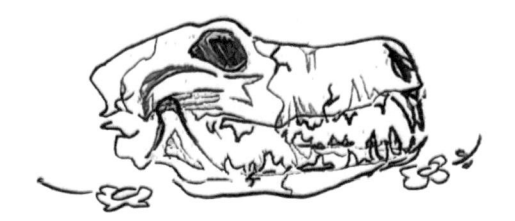

To walk in nature is to witness a thousand miracles." – Marie Davis

Among the Green, Cherish Brown, Photography

Homelessness

Diamond Kumani

I remember the day my mom sat me and my brother down holding tears in her eyes to tell us that we had to move. It was June of 2013. My mom had been ill for a while and I was only seven and my brother was nine. I was scared and I didn't know where we were going to go.

We ended up at my grandmother's little apartment where three, periodically four, people lived. The fourth was my cousin who is six months older than me. She would get kicked out of her house and stay there with her dad who is also my uncle. This time was difficult and everything felt out of place. We had taken the room of my other older cousin Trinity. She had lived with my grandma since she was a baby because her mom and her grandma, who is one of my grandma's eight sisters, couldn't take care of her.

Trin had written notes to us saying that "she was happy to have us here and she gave us her room because she knew it was a hard time for us." During this time I tried to hide the fact that I was

> "The shadow I mourned came back, but it had been replaced by a big dark and stormy rain cloud and a heavy weight."

homeless, a sentence not many can say at the age of seven. I cried, constantly knowing that I did not have a home to go back to.

Whilst I had to hide the fact that I was homeless from the world I had to deal with losing my mom. My mom isn't dead. I lost her as a mom and gained a shadow in the night that would kiss me and my brother and then go sleep in the car; a shadow that wasn't around but for mere moments. Ironically, I chose the word "shadow" because a shadow is always there behind you. But mine was gone.

Without my mom there I had to learn independence fast. I already had found some type of independence because I had to take care of myself while she was ill. I didn't understand at the time the gravity of my situation. I thought all kids took care of themselves, as well as their moms, grandmothers, and baby cousins. I thought that all kids knew how to cook full thanksgiving dinners and how to change dirty, stinky diapers. Because that was all I knew.

I grew up with the knowledge that everything can be taken away and the only person who's gonna get you somewhere is you. So due to this belief I became extremely hard on myself to become the perfect child. Perfect grades, perfect looks. Everything perfect. Oh, how I wish I could go back and tell myself to breathe, that I was good enough no matter what, and that my hard times would be the thing to make me strong.

By the time I was in third grade, taking care of people and finding spare moments to have real childhood fun was normal for me. See, living with grandma wasn't all bad. It allowed me to be closer to my cousins, and I found my love for music, food, dance, animals, and nature. Me and my cousins and my brother would create creative cheerful songs and difficult dances. We endured together. We shared our fears and hopes for life, and we helped each other create our own little world where the real world responsibilities couldn't even be imagined. True friendship, even though we are all related, our moments together created a true friendship between us.

I lived with my grandmother for two years. I was in third grade. By now I was set into my normal routine when one day my mom offered to take me and my brother to school. But I found it unusual because my grandma had come along and my mom was driving nowhere near the school. Also me and my brother usually took the bus. While trying to figure out where we were going and vigorously asking my mother questions about our destination, I had fallen asleep.

When I woke up I was at a townhouse. The numbers on the house were "6478," my new house—a new start. But what I didn't know is that this house would give me my greatest joys and also be the place where my darkest fears would soon come true. Dec 11 and June 27 are two different years but also two horrible days. I lost my baby cousin on Dec 11 2016 around 9 pm, and it changed my family's life forever. Her name was Gianni, and she was only two years old. She was one of the greatest lights of our family and we will forever miss our lady bug. The new house also had given me joyous moments like my first room, my first nerf gun war, my first water war, my first pet, and my first crush.

It's taken me a long time to erase this notion from my mind. It's caused me to overwork myself, leading to burnout in high school that brought me back to the very moment the notion was placed to be true in my head. Pain, torment—those are the only words I could use to describe the feeling. The constant "YOU ARE NOT GOOD ENOUGH." The shadow I mourned came back, but it had been replaced by a big dark and stormy rain cloud and a heavyweight.

I take pride in my experiences in life, and I give all the glory of getting through them to God and our family's strength, especially my mom. I could not erase the past, I wouldn't if I could. My experiences have created a beautiful young lady that will grow into an experienced, hardworking, grateful woman. I will continue to grow and allow my life to inspire me to keep going.

The Melting Faces
By Ryan Fonjock

Distance

Serena Morin

I look out at the moon
Staring and taking in its beauty
Hoping we're staring at the same time
Wishing we were in the same place
But at the end of the day there's just space
Between us
Around us
Circling us
But I think about it this way
Distance means so little
When a person means so much

"With every step in nature's depth, She was becoming more herself." – Angie Welland-Crosby

Coral Bells, Victoria Cameron Photography

Advisor Letter

Now I understand what my high school literary magazine advisor, Mrs. Snyder, meant by the lit mag process becoming a little more difficult each year. This year, here at North County, was no different. This year we lost Knight Time, which cut into a lot of our progress. The literary magazine class was taught by another teacher and most of the staff was not enrolled in the class, which also cut into our progress. Part of the lit mag meetings were held virtually, in order to make our deadline. Submissions were slow and few and far between. The things that worked in our favor, however, was a high staff turnout and some really talented writers and artists on the staff. The passion in this group of individuals is every Advisor's dream, and it is because of them that this year's volume even happened.

A huge thank you to Dr. Melinda Lasher for her support of the literary magazine and purchasing items needed for next year's publication. The staff is very appreciative and are so excited to create even better lit mags in the future. Dr. Lasher, we love you!

Rose, thank you for four years of working on and supporting the lit mag. The staff sends you off into adulthood with love and good vibes.

To our newbies who stepped up and worked dilligently

Staff Page

Our Leader
Victoria Cameron

Editor-in-Chief
Rose Dorsch

Assistant Editor-in-Chief
Serena Morin

Literary Editor
Riley Miller-Hubbard

Designer
Cherish "Meatball" Brown
Victoria Cameron
Alivia Houghtling

Art Team
Waverly Boyer
Emily Gonzales
Chloe Heslop
Angel Jimenez
Madelyn Moss

Literary Team
Seth Black
Mykala Brown
Malaya Campbell
Alaina Cousin
Kendra Ferrell
Sydeny Jones
Vanessa Jones
Alayna Linsenmeyer
JaWaun McFaddon

Marketing
Ka'den "Noodle" Clea
Reese Kiser
Kaylee Ludwing
Keiry Penado
Airiana Taylor

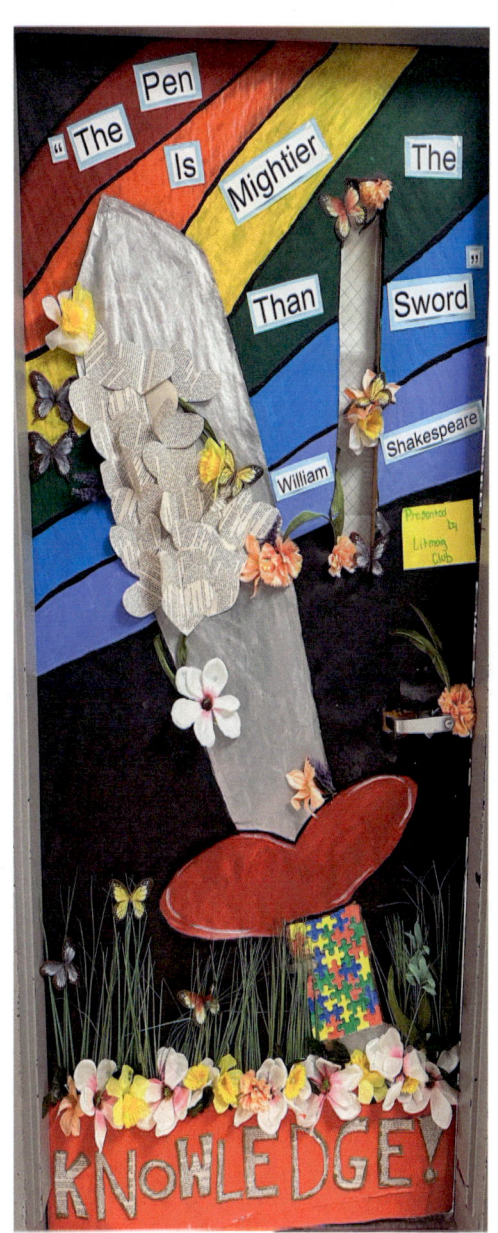

Ms. Cameron's classroom door, created by the lit mag club

Philosophy

Different shades of green represent our earth and the damage we've done. We as people need to change perspectives and think of the life that surrounds us. We've been blinded by society, therefore, we have not taken the time and consideration to fully grasp the harm caused by us.

Vines and plants on the page that eventually are out as humans and the negligence comes to pass. Red and yellow incorporated as we progress and the season's change.

Ordering darker pieces later in the magazine and optimistic pieces earlier match the changing tone and emotion of our natural world. In between sections you will notice the cover art upside down. This represents how our world has been flipped upside down from humans, and it is our duty to our planet to do better and be better.

No Title Given, Buka Ragu, Mixed Media

Made in the USA
Columbia, SC
11 May 2024